The Sayings of W.B. Yeats

GW00320198

The Sayings of

W.B.
YEATS

edited by
JOSEPH SPENCE

Duckworth

First published in 1993 by
Gerald Duckworth & Co. Ltd.
The Old Piano Factory
48 Hoxton Square
London N1 6PB
Tel: 071 729 5986
Fax: 071 729 0015

Introduction and editorial arrangement
© 1993 by Joseph Spence

ISBN 0 7156 2457 1

A catalogue record for this book is available
from the British Library

Typeset by Ray Davies
Printed in Great Britain by
Redwood Press Limited, Melksham

Contents

For

Roy Foster

Introduction

So distinctive is the style or purpose of some of the great Irish writers that they have bequeathed to us adjectives which are as well known as their works. People who have never read Swift, Wilde, Shaw or Joyce can, nevertheless, readily employ the terms Swiftian, Wildean, Shavian and Joycean. It would be a bold reader of the work of William Butler Yeats (1865-1939) who would use the term 'Yeatsian', without offering a personal definition of it. The question of 'the identity of Yeats' has challenged all his biographers.

Yeats was Irish Renaissance Man, both as a pioneer of the Irish literary revival of the 1890s and in the range of his artistic and public activities. But this does not fully explain the problem of establishing his identity. What clouds the issue further is that Yeats, to use his own words, often sought to 'remake' or 'renew' himself. As a poet he was the last of the romantics, a national bard, an early symbolist and a sometime realist. In the theatre he was equally proud of his promotion of the mystical drama of the Celtic Twilight and of his administrative acumen: 'theatre business, management of men' being a hard labour which proved 'the fascination of what's difficult'. As a public man he was an Irish nationalist and the enemy of all politicisers of nationalism; a shy and courteous citizen of the post-heroic twentieth century and a fierce and radical anti-modernist. He was a liberal on the issue of artistic licence, but a conservative on many other questions, until, in his later years, excited by Fascism as a social doctrine.

Yeats, who as a poet progressed from bohemian dreamer to national magus, was also a notable essayist, playwright, theatre manager, theosophist, folklorist and statesman. He was a man of many masks and a great myth maker: an inventor of traditions and, as W.J. McCormack has it, 'a formidable reviser of history'. The history Yeats revised most successfully was his own. He was born into a professional Dublin Protestant family, but he also portrayed himself as a descendant of a proud, provincial, merchant Ireland, inhabited by 'half-legendary men' (his Sligo ancestors, the Pollexfens and Middletons) and as a latter-day apostle of a great European aristocracy, the Protestant Ascendancy, that class of Irishmen of English descent whom he came to identify as the Anglo-Irish.

That Yeats should have offered these alternative ancestries reveals a certain insecurity as to where he belonged in Ireland which remained until very near the end of his life. In his early poem 'To Ireland in Coming Times', he wrote: 'Know, that I would accounted be/ True brother of a company/ That sang, to sweeten Ireland's wrong,/ Ballad and story, rann and song.' Thereafter, Yeats was to declare himself an associate of many companies – political, aesthetic and spiritual – but he tended to grow disillusioned when they failed to match his idealised vision of them. This had artistic benefits, however, for, to adapt one of Yeats's own sayings, he made his prose out of arguments with others who failed him; his poetry out of a failure to live up to his own ideals.

Always disappointed by compromise, Yeats's heroes were men and women who appeared impervious to common criticism and changing times. This explains the respect he had for the martyrs of the 'terrible beauty' of the 1916 Dublin Rising, who proved that they lived beyond 'where motley is worn'. It also explains his admiration for idealists, like his father and John Millington Synge, who put their art before fortune or friendship, and for pure patriots, like John O'Leary, who taught him that there could be no nationality without literature, no great literature without nationality. This is not to suggest that Yeats made his art out of a celebration of plaster saints. The vices of Maud Gonne, Yeats's chief muse from their first meeting, when he was twenty-three, inspired the poet as often as her virtues. However, when the flesh and blood Maud disappointed him, Yeats would tend to transmogrify her into Helen of Troy, the ideal of human beauty, or Cathleen ni Houlihan, the personification of an Ireland suffering only to be reborn. Thus idealism rose phoenix-like out of the ashes of a lost reputation.

Yeats wrote constantly about old age and about his feelings for particular places. From 1889, when he published *The Wanderings of Oisin*, old age was an important subject of his poetry, and for nearly fifty years he wrote poignantly, and prophetically, of the fact that he would find no solace in age, but remain as full of longing, as concerned to remake himself, as he had ever been. From equally early on in his life, Yeats had identified a succession of certain sacred places, notably Sligo, Lady Gregory's Coole Park and Thoor Ballylee, as havens from a world of commerce and the commonplace. Some of his most memorable poetry was crafted out of his longing for these rural idylls, but Yeats lived most of his life in London and Dublin, alternately exhilarated and exasperated by the restlessness of the city. He did live at Thoor Ballylee, the tower he built in County Galway, for a short time in the 1920s, but it remained for him a symbol of the poet's stand against the 'filthy modern tide' rather than a home. It was also the only estate Yeats ever owned, so it was important in a physical sense, because it allowed him to perceive himself as associated with the tradition of the Irish landed gentry.

Other 'traditions' were established in the same way. The evocation of the 'half-legendary men' of Sligo enabled him to create a familial tradition, while he created a national tradition out of his eulogies and elegies for Romantic Ireland and out of a fusion of a mythical Celtic past and an actual Irish present. On whether his own work belonged to a tradition he was more ambivalent. He once declared that art transcended tradition, being beyond place and history, but he also wrote, in one of his earliest autobiographical essays, that one of his lifelong objectives was to make of his art 'an infallible Church of poetic tradition'.

The most influential tradition Yeats invented was the Anglo-Irish tradition. That Ireland owed a great debt to the illustrious Protestant Irishmen of the eighteenth century was an idea popularised in the late nineteenth century by the historian W.E.H. Lecky, but it was Yeats who went on to the offensive on behalf of Anglo-Ireland. In 1925, frustrated by the determination of the Irish Free State government to incorporate Catholic social doctrine into its constitution, he declared that his heritage was that of the Irish Protestant people of Swift, Grattan and Parnell, who were 'no petty people', but one of the great stocks of Europe.

Why Yeats promoted the cause of the Anglo-Irish when he did reveals how he could 'remake' himself at will. From the mid-1920s he portrayed Protestant Ireland as an intellectual Arcadia and had Swift, Berkeley, Goldsmith, Burke and Grattan depicted as the enemies of 'Whiggery' – a shorthand for English materialism and rationalism. He had once dismissed some of these characters as being hardly Irish at all, but with the establishment of the new Free State as a Catholic state, he recreated the myth of Protestant Ireland and portrayed himself as one of its leading characters. Reflecting that Mother Ireland seemed to have disowned her best sons he remade his national heritage and declared himself to be one of those great Anglo-Irish 'solitaries' who were greater than their age and who stood apart from the mere Catholic Irish.

Ultimately Yeats threw off the craving to belong to a company and portrayed himself above the causes and movements of his age, as Swift had been and as those other great Anglo-Irishmen, G.B. Shaw and Oscar Wilde, were in his own time. It was the pride he took in Protestant individualism, therefore, that enabled Yeats, a great creator and hater of systems, to release himself from his long quest for a personal system and all-encompassing tradition. Only at the end of his life did he begin to see himself as others were already seeing him – as a great but solitary genius.

Childhood & Youth

I think I confused my grandfather [William Pollexfen] with God, for I remember in one of my attacks of melancholy praying that he might punish me for my sins ... Even today when I read King Lear his image is always before me, and I wonder if the delight in passionate men in my plays and in my poetry is more than his memory.

Reveries over Childhood and Youth, 1914

When I was ten or twelve my father took me to see Irving play Hamlet ... For many years Hamlet was an image of heroic self-possession for the poses of youth and childhood to copy, a combatant of the battle within myself.   *Ib.*

I began to play at being a sage, a magician or a poet. I had many idols ... but I soon chose Alastor for my chief of men and longed to share his melancholy, and maybe at last to disappear from everybody's sight as he disappeared drifting in a boat along some slow moving river between great trees.   *Ib.*

I wished to become self-possessed, to be able to play with hostile minds as Hamlet played, to look in the lion's face as it were, with unquivering eyelash ... I did not discover that Hamlet had his self-possession from no schooling but from indifference and passion-conquering sweetness, and that less heroic minds can but hope for it from old age.   *Ib.*

We were merchant people of the town. No matter how rich we grew, no matter how many thousands a year our mills or our ships brought in, we could never be 'county', nor indeed had we any desire to be so. We would meet on grand juries those people in the great houses ... and we would speak no malicious gossip and knew ourselves respected in turn, but the long-settled habit of Irish life set up a wall.

'Autobiography', 1916-17

At seventeen years old I was already an old-fashioned brass cannon full of shot, and nothing had kept me from going off but a doubt as to my capacity to shoot straight.

The Trembling of the Veil, 1922

I was unlike others of my generation in one thing only. I am very religious, and deprived by Huxley and Tyndall, whom I detested, of the simple-minded religion of my childhood, I had made a new religion, almost an infallible Church of poetic tradition.

Ib.

Experience

My life has been in my poems ... I have seen others enjoying, while I stand alone with myself – commenting, commenting – a mere dead mirror on which things reflect themselves.

Letter to Katharine Tynan, 1888

I always knew that the line of Nature is crooked, that, though we dig the canal-beds as straight as we can, the rivers run hither and thither in their wildness.

'What is Popular Poetry?', 1901

Is not all life the struggle of experience, naked, unarmed,
timid but immortal, against generalised thought?
'Journal', August 1910

All life weighed in the scales of my own life seems to me
a preparation for something that never happens.
Reveries over Childhood and Youth, 1914

If we cannot imagine ourselves as different from what
we are, and try to assume that second self, we cannot
impose a discipline upon ourselves though we may
accept one from others. Active virtue, as distinguished
from the passive acceptance of a code, is therefore
theatrical, consciously dramatic, the wearing of a mask.
Per Amica Silentia Lunae, 1917

We begin to live when we conceive life as tragedy.
The Trembling of the Veil, 1922

I know now that revelation is from the self, but from that
age-long memoried self, that shapes the elaborate shell
of the mollusc and the child in the womb, that teaches
the birds to make their nest; and that genius is a crisis
that joins that buried self for certain moments to our
trivial daily mind.   *Ib.*

Women

When I thought of women they were modelled on those
in my favourite poets and loved in brief tragedy, or like
the girl in *The Revolt of Islam*, accompanied their lovers
through all manner of wild places, lawless women
without homes and without children.
Reveries over Childhood and Youth, 1914

Their hearts are wild,/ As the hearts of birds, till children come.

The Land of Heart's Desire, 1894

You are the best woman in Ireland, but money is good, too. *Cathleen ni Houlihan*, 1902

Yet they that know all things but know
That all this life can give us is
A child's laughter, a woman's kiss.

Baile and Aillinn, 1903

What woman is there that a man can trust
But at the moment when he kisses her
At the first midnight?

Deirdre, 1907

May God be praised for woman
That gives up all her mind,
A man may find in no man
A friendship of her kind
That covers all he has brought
As with her flesh and bone,
Nor quarrels with a thought
Because it is not her own. 'On Woman', 1914

It's certain that fine women eat
A crazy salad with their meat
Thereby the Horn of Plenty is undone.

'A Prayer for my Daughter', 1919

The Queen. Men hold
  That woman's beauty is a kindly thing,
  But they that call me cruel speak the truth,
  Cruel as the winter of virginity.

A Full Moon in March, 1935

Maud Gonne

I was twenty-three years old when the troubling of my life began … I had never thought to see in living woman so great beauty. It belonged to famous pictures, to poetry, to some legendary past.

'Autobiography', *c.* 1916-17

I knew that my friends had all mistresses of one kind or another and that most, at need, went home with harlots … I had never since childhood kissed a woman's lips. At Hammersmith I saw a woman of the town walking up and down in the empty railway station. I thought of offering myself to her, but the old thought came back, 'No, I love the most beautiful woman in the world.'

Autobiography, c. 1916-17

Today the thought came to me that [she] never really understands my plans, or nature, or ideas. Then came the thought, what matter? How much the best I have done and still do is but an attempt to explain myself to her?

'Journal', January 1909

I had this thought a while ago,
'My darling cannot understand
What I have done, or what would do
In this blind bitter land.'

'Words', 1909

[I think] of her … as in a sense Ireland, a summing up in one mind of what is best in the romantic political Ireland of my youth and of the youth of others for some years yet.

'Journal', May 1910

A woman Homer sung,
That life and letters seem
But an heroic dream.

'A Woman Homer Sung', 1910

Yet she, singing upon her road,
Half lion, half child, is at peace.

'Against Unworthy Praise', 1910

A young man when the old men are done talking
Will say to an old man, 'Tell me of that lady
The poet stubborn with his passion sang us
When age might have chilled his blood.'

'Broken Dreams', 1915

They had read
All I had rhymed of that monstrous thing
Returned and yet unrequited love.

'Presences', 1915

An intellectual hatred is the worst,
So let her think opinions are accursed.
Have I not seen the loveliest woman born
Out of the mouth of Plenty's horn,
Because of her opinionated mind
Barter that horn and every good
By quiet natures understood
For an old bellows full of angry wind?

'A Prayer for my Daughter', 1919

She smiled and that transfigured me
And left me but a lout,
Maundering here and maundering there,
Emptier of thought
Than the heavenly curcuit of its stars
When the moon sails out.

'A Man Young and Old', 1927

Maud Gonne at Howth station waiting a train,
Pallas Athene in that straight back and arrogant head:
All the Olympians; a thing never known again.

'Beautiful Lofty Things', *c.* 1937

Love

Although our love is waning, let us stand
By the lone border of the lake once more,
Together in that hour of gentleness
When the poor tired child, Passion, falls asleep.

'Ephemera', 1884

They were such good friends they had never fallen in
love with each other. Perfect love and perfect friendship
are indeed incompatible, for the one is a battlefield
where shadows war beside the combatants, and the
other a placid country where Consultation has her
dwelling.   *John Sherman*, 1891

Love is based on inequality as friendship is on equality.

Ib.

Who mocks at music mocks at love.

The Countess Cathleen, 1892

While they danced there came over them the weariness
with the world, the melancholy, the pity one for the
other, which is the exultation of love.

The Secret Rose, 1897

It seems to me that love, if fine, is essentially a discipline.

'Journal', January 1909

Love is created and preserved by intellectual analysis,
for we love only that which is unique, and it belongs to
contemplation, not to action, for we would not change
that which we love.   *A Vision*, 1937

Wine comes in at the mouth
And love comes in at the eye;
That's all we shall know for truth
Before we grow old and die.
I lift the glass to my mouth,
I look at you, and I sigh.   'A Drinking Song', 1910

Places

All the well-known families had their grotesque or tragic
or romantic legends, and I often said to myself how
terrible it would be to go away and die where nobody
would know my story. Years afterwards, when I was ten
or twelve years old and in London, I would remember
Sligo with tears, and when I began to write, it was there
I hoped to find my audience.

Reveries over Childhood and Youth, 1914

I remember when we were children how intense our
devotion was to all things in Sligo and still see in my
mother the old feeling.   Letter to Katharine Tynan, 1891

Any breath from Ireland blows pleasurably in this
hateful London where you cannot go five paces without
seeing some wretched object broken either by wealth or
poverty.   Letter to Katharine Tynan, 1887

A faint mist half covered away the houses and factory
chimneys on the further side; beside him a band of
osiers swayed softly, the deserted and full river lapping
their stems. He looked on all these things with foreign
eyes. He had no sense of possession. Indeed it seemed to
him that everything in London was owned by too many
to be owned by any one.

John Sherman, 1891

I will arise and go now, and go to Innisfree,
And a small cabin build there, of clay and wattles made:
Nine bean-rows will I have there, a hive for the
   honey-bee,
And live alone in the bee-loud glade.

'The Lake Isle of Innisfree', 1888

Jonathan Swift made a soul for the gentlemen of this city
[Dublin] by hating his neighbour as himself.

The Tables of the Law, 1897

How should the world be luckier if this house,
Where passion and precision have been one
Time out of mind, became too ruinous
To breed the lidless eye that loves the sun?

[On Coole] 'Upon a House shaken by the Land Agitation', 1909

I am making a setting for my old age, a place to
influence lawless youth, with its severity and antiquity.

Letter to John Quinn, 1918

I, the poet William Yeats,
With old mill boards and sea-green slates,
And smithy work from the Gort forge,
Restored this tower for my wife George;
And may these characters remain
When all is ruin once again.

'To be Carved on a Stone at Thoor Ballylee', 1918

God grant a blessing on this tower and cottage
And on my heirs, if all remain unspoiled,
No table or chair or stool not simple enough
For shepherd lads in Galilee ...
         and should some limb of the Devil
Destroy the view by cutting down an ash
That shades the road, or setting up a cottage
Planned in a government office, shorten his life,
Manacle his soul upon the Red Sea bottom.

'A Prayer on going into my House', 1918

We are on the bridge; that shadow is the tower,
And the light proves that he is reading still.
He has found, after the manner of his kind,
Mere images; chosen this place to live in
Because, it may be, of the candle-light
From the far tower where Milton's Platonist
Sat late, or Shelley's visionary prince:
The lonely light that Samuel Palmer engraved,
An image of mysterious wisdom won by toil;
And now he seeks in book or manuscript
What he shall never find.

'The Phases of the Moon', 1918

Blessed be this place,
More blessed still this tower;
A bloody arrogant power
Rose out of the race
Uttering, mastering it,
Rose like these walls from these
Storm-beaten cottages –
In mockery I have set
A powerful emblem up,
And sing it rhyme upon rhyme
In mockery of a time
Half dead at the top.

'Blood and the Moon', 1927

Old Age

An old man stirs the fire to a blaze,
In the house of a child, of a friend, of a brother.
He has over-lingered his welcome; the days
Grown desolate, whisper and sigh to each other;
He hears the storm in the chimney above,
And bends to the fire and shakes with the cold,
While his heart still dreams of battle and love,
And the cry of the hounds on the hills of old.

The Wanderings of Oisin, 1889

Ah me! to be shaken with coughing and broken with old
   age and pain,
Without laughter, a show unto children, alone with
   remembrance and fear;
All emptied of purple hours as a beggar's cloak in the
   rain,
As a hay-cock out on the flood, or a wolf sucked under a
   weir.   *Ib.*

There's not a woman turns her face
Upon a broken tree,
And yet the beauties that I loved
Are in my memory;
I spit into the face of Time
That has transfigured me.

'The Lamentation of the Old Pensioner', 1890

There is always something in our enemy that we like,
and something in our sweetheart that we dislike. It is
this entanglement of moods which makes us old, and
puckers our brows and deepens the furrows about our
eyes.   *The Celtic Twilight*, 1893

We have given the world our passion,
We have naught for death but toys.

'Upon a Dying Lady', *c.* 1912-14

I thought no more was needed
Youth to prolong
Than dumb-bell and foil
To keep the body young.
O who could have foretold
That the heart grows old?

'A Song', 1915

Bald heads forgetful of their sins,
Old, learned, respectable bald heads
Edit and annonate the lines
That young men, tossing on their beds,
Rhymed out in love's despair
To flatter beauty's ignorant ear.

'The Scholars', 1915

The holy centaurs of the hills are vanished;
I have nothing but the embittered sun;
Banished heroic mother moon and vanished,
And now that I have come to fifty years
I must endure the timid sun.

'Lines Written in Dejection', 1915

Who but an idiot would praise / A withered tree?
At the Hawk's Well, 1917

Much did I rage when young,
Being by the world oppressed,
But now with flattering tongue
It speeds the parting guest.

'Youth and Age', 1924

What shall I do with this absurdity –
O heart, O troubled heart – this caricature,
Decrepit age that has been tied to me
As to a dog's tail? ...
Did all old men and women, rich and poor,
Who trod upon these rocks or passed this door,
Whether in public or in secret rage
As I do now against old age?

'The Tower', 1925

I feel constantly if I were but twenty years old and not
over sixty all I ever wanted to do could be done easily.
One never tires of life and at the last one must die of
thirst with the cup at one's lips.

Letter to H.G.C. Grierson, 1926

An aged man is but a paltry thing,
A tattered coat upon a stick, unless
Soul claps its hands and sing.

'Sailing to Byzantium', 1926

Once out of Irish bitterness I can find some measure of
sweetness and light, as befits old age – already new
poems are floating in my head, bird songs of an old
man, joy in the passing moment, emotion without the
bitterness of memory.

Letter to Olivia Shakespear, 1928

Endure what life God gives and ask no longer span;
Cease to remember the delights of youth, travel-wearied
     ancient man;
Delight becomes death-longing if all longing else be vain.

Sophocles' Oedipus at Colonus, 1934

I pray – for fashion's word is out
And prayer comes round again –
That I may seem, though I die old,
A foolish, passionate man.

'A Prayer for Old Age', 1934

Now his wars on God begin;
At the stroke of midnight God shall win.

'The Four Ages of Man', 1934

Grant me an old man's frenzy,
Myself I must remake
Till I am Timon and Lear
Or that William Blake
Who beat upon the wall
Till truth obeyed his call.

'An Acre of Grass', 1936

'The work is done,' grown old he thought,
'According to my boyish plan;
Let the fools rage, I swerved in naught,
Something to perfection brought';
But louder sang that ghost, 'What then?'

'What Then?', 1936

You think it horrible that lust and rage
Should dance attention upon my old age;
They were not such a plague when I was young;
What else have I to spur me into song?

'The Spur', 1936

I must lie down where all the ladders start,
In the foul rag-and-bone shop of the heart.

'The Circus Animals' Desertion', 1937-8

I know for certain my time will not be long. I have put
away everything that can be put away that I may speak
what I have to speak … When I try to put all into a
phrase I say, 'Man can embody truth but he cannot
know it.' I must embody it in the completion of my life.
The abstract is not life and everywhere draws out its
contradictions. You can refute Hegel but not the Saints
or the Song of Sixpence.

Letter to Lady Elizabeth Pelham, 4 January 1939

Poetry

Words are always getting conventionalised to some
secondary meaning. It is one of the works of poetry to
take the truants in custody and bring them back to their
right senses. Poets are the policemen of language, they
are always arresting those old rebrobates the words.

Letter to Ellen O'Leary, 1889

All poetry should have a local habitation when at all
possible.
Letter to Katharine Tynan, 1889

His intellect was like a musician's instrument without a
sounding-board. He could think carefully and cleverly,
and even with originality, but never in such a way as to
make his thoughts an allusion to something deeper than
themselves. In this he was the reverse of poetical, for
poetry is essentially a touch from behind the curtain.
John Sherman, 1891

It was only with the modern poets, with Goethe and
Wordsworth and Browning, that poetry gave up the
right to consider all things in the world as a dictionary of
types and symbols and began to call itself a critic of life
and an interpreter of things as they are.
'The Autumn of the Body', 1898

Beauty is the end and law of poetry.
Letter to George Russell (AE), 1900

Better to go down upon your marrow-bones
And scrub a kitchen pavement, or break stones
Like an old pauper, in all kinds of weather;
For to articulate sweet sounds together
Is to work harder than all these, and yet
Be thought an idler by the noisy set
Of bankers, schoolmasters, and clergymen
The martyrs call the world.
'Adam's Curse', 1901

And I would have all know that when all falls
In ruin, poetry calls out in joy,
Being the scattering hand, the bursting pod,
The victim's joy among the holy flame,
God's laughter at the shattering of the world.
The King's Threshold (1904)

The poet's enemies are those industries that make the
good citizen. A poet is a good citizen turned inside out.
'Journal', January 1909

We must not leave our garrets, but we could not write
well but for what we see from the windows.   *Ib.*

All things can tempt me from this craft of verse:
One time it was a woman's face, or worse –
The seeming needs of my fool-driven land;
Now nothing but comes readier to the hand
Than this accustomed toil. When I was young
I had not given a penny for a song
Did not the poet sing it with such airs
That one believed he had a sword upstairs;
Yet would be now, could I but have my wish,
Colder and dumber and deafer than a fish.

'All Things can Tempt me', 1908

We should write out our own thoughts in as nearly as
possible the language we thought them in, as though in
a letter to an intimate friend.

Reveries over Childhood and Youth, 1914

I think it better that in times like these
A poet's mouth be silent, for in truth
We have no gift to set a statesman right;
He has had enough of meddling who can please
A young girl in the indolence of her youth,
Or an old man upon a winter's night.

'On being asked for a War Poem', 1915

We make out of the quarrel with others, rhetoric, but out
of the quarrel with ourselves, poetry.

Per Amica Silentia Lunae, 1917

A poet is justified not by the expression of himself, but
by the public he finds or creates; a public made by
others ready to his hand if he is a mere popular poet, but
a new public, a new form of life, if he is a man of genius.

Introduction to *Essays and Introductions*, 1937

A poet writes always of his personal life, in his finest
work out of its tragedy, whatever it be, remorse, lost
love, or mere loneliness; he never speaks directly as to
someone at the breakfast table, there is always a
phantasmagoria.

'A General Introduction for my Work', 1937

Seek those images
That constitute the wild,
The lion and the virgin,
The harlot and the child.
Find in middle air
An eagle on the wing,
Recognise the five
That make the Muses sing.   'Those Images', 1937

Art & Literature

He was at the marchland between waking and dreaming
where our thoughts begin to have a life of their own –
the region where art is nurtured and inspiration born.
John Sherman, 1891

In France literature divides itself into schools,
movements, and circles ... In England ... each man
works by himself and for himself, for England is the
land of literary Ishmaels.

'The Celt in London', 1892

Art and poetry, by constantly using symbolism,
constantly remind us that nature itself is a symbol. To
remember this, is to be redeemed from nature's death
and destruction. This is Blake's message.

Preface to *The Works of William Blake*, 1893

False art is not expressive, but mimetic, not from experience but from observation, and is the mother of all evil, persuading us to save our bodies alive at no matter what cost of rapine and fraud.

'William Blake and his Illustrations to the *Divine Comedy*', 1897

All folk literature, and all literature that keeps the folk tradition, delights in unbounded and immoral things ... All folk literature has indeed a passion whose life is not in modern literature and music and art, except where it has come by some straight or crooked way out of ancient times.

'The Celtic Element in Literature', 1897

The arts are, I believe, about to take upon their shoulders the burdens that have fallen from the shoulders of priests, and to lead us back upon our journey by filling our thoughts with the essence of things, and not with things. We are about to substitute once more the distillation of alchemy for the analyses of chemistry.

'The Autumn of the Body', 1898

In my heart of hearts I have never been quite certain that one should be more than an artist, that even patriotism is more than an impure desire in an artist.

'What is Popular Poetry', 1901

[Art] brings us near to the archetypal ideas themselves, and away from nature, which is but their looking-glass.

'At Stratford-on-Avon', May 1901

I believe that literature is the principal voice of the conscience, and it is its duty age after age to affirm its morality against the specific moralities of clergymen and churches; and of kings and parliaments and peoples.

Letter to the Editor of the *Freeman's Journal*, 14 November 1901

Folk-art is, indeed, the oldest of the aristocracies of thought, and because it refuses what is passing and trivial, the merely clever and pretty, as certainly as the vulgar and insincere, and because it has gathered into itself the simplest and most unforgettable thoughts of the generations, it is the soil where all great art is rooted.

The Celtic Twilight, 1901

We who care deeply about the arts find ourselves the priesthood of an almost forgotten faith, and we must, I think, if we would win the people again, take upon ourselves the method and the fervour of a priesthood. We must be half humble and half proud. ...We must baptize as well as preach.   'Ireland and the Arts', 1901

The Catholic Church is not the less the Church of the people because the mass is spoken in Latin, and art is not less the art of the people because it does not speak in the language they are used to.   *Ib.*

Even the highest political motives will not make an artist.

'Journal', January 1909

Opinion ... is the enemy of the artist because it arms his uninspired moment against his inspiration.

'Journal', February 1909

A mind without traditional culture, moral or literary, is only powerful to hate.   *Ib.*

The mood of creation is very fragile.

'Journal', March 1909

All literature created out of a conscious political aim ... creates weakness by creating a habit of unthinking obedience and a habit of distrust of spontaneous impulse. It makes a nation of slaves in the name of liberty.   'Journal', May 1910.

All good art is experience; all popular bad art generalisation.

'Journal', August 1910

All art is a disengaging of a soul from place and history.
'J.M. Synge and the Ireland of his Time', 1910

Works of art are always begotten by previous works of
art, and every masterpiece becomes the Abraham of a
chosen people. 'Art and Ideas', 1913

A good writer should be so simple that he has no faults,
only sins. 'Journal', October 1914

It is not permitted to a man who takes up pen or chisel,
to seek originality, for passion is his only business, and
he cannot but mould or sing after a new fashion because
no disaster is like another.
Per Amica Silentia Lunae, 1917

Whether we have chosen chisel, pen or brush,
We are but critics, or but half-create,
Timid, entangled, empty and abashed,
Lacking the countenance of our friends.
'Ego Dominus Tuus', 1915

I think you can leave the arts, superior or inferior, to the
general conscience of mankind.
Senate Speech on Censorship of Films, 1923

The romantic movement with its turbulent heroism, its
self-assertion, is over, superseded by a new naturalism
that leaves man helpless before the contents of his own
mind. 'Bishop Berkeley', July 1931

The public does not matter – only one's friends matter.
Letter to Edith Shackleton Heald, 18 May 1937

We writers are public opinion's children though we defy our mother.   'To Ezra Pound', 1928, in *A Vision*, 1937

Literary heroes & villains

Neither Christ nor Buddha nor Socrates wrote a book, for to do that is to exchange life for a logical process.
Estrangement, 1909

I feel in Hamlet, as always in Shakespeare, that I am in the presence of a soul lingering on the storm-beaten threshold of sanctity. Has not that threshold always been terrible, even crime-haunted?
'Journal', October 1909

When a country produces a man of genius he never is what it wants or believes it wants, he is always unlike its idea of itself. In the eighteenth century Scotland believed itself very religious and very moral and very gloomy, and its national poet Burns came not to speak of these things but to speak of lust and drink and drunken gaiety.
'Journal', April 1909

The fruit of Robert Burns and Scott with their lack of ideas, their external and picturesque view of life, has been to create not a nation but a province with a sense of the picturesque.
'Journal', May 1910

Sir Walter Scott gave Highland legends and Highland excitability so great a mastery over all romance that they seem romance itself.
'The Celtic Element in Literature', 1897

William Blake was the first writer of modern times to preach the indissoluble marriage of all great art with symbol.
'William Blake and his Illustrations to the *Divine Comedy*', 1897

I ... made [Shelley's] Prometheus Unbound my sacred book.
Reveries over Childhood and Youth, 1914

Carleton and Banim ... Griffin and Kickham ... tried to
make one see life plainly but all written down in a kind
of fiery shorthand that it might never be forgotten.

Letter to Fr Matthew Russell, 1889

William Carleton was a great Irish historian. The history
of a nation is not in parliaments and battlefields, but in
what people say to each other on fair days and high
days, and in how they farm, and quarrel, and go on
pilgrimage. These things Carleton has recorded.

Introduction to *Stories from Carleton*, 1889

Great literature has always been written in a ... spirit
[of] Forgiveness of Sin, and when we find it becoming
the Accusation of Sin, as in George Eliot ... literature has
begun to become something else.

'At Stratford-on-Avon', May 1901

The Russians make us debate some point of view
peculiar to the author, Flaubert etherealises all with his
conviction that life is no better than a smell of cooking
through a grating. But Balzac leaves us when the book is
closed amid the crowd that fills the boxes and the
galleries of grand opera.   'Louis Lambert', July 1934

To Robert Browning the world was simply a great
boarding house in which people come and go in a
confused kind of way. The clatter and the chatter to him
was life, was joy itself. Sometimes the noise and
restlessness got too much into his poetry, and the
expression became confused and the verse splintered
and broken.   'The Celt in London', *Boston Pilot*, 1890

Longfellow has his popularity, in the main, because he
tells his story or his idea so that one needs nothing but
his verses to understand it.

'What is "Popular Poetry"?', 1901

Swinburne has been these many years, if we consider his
verse alone, too careful of the sound, too careless of the
sense.

Letter to the Editor of *The Bookman*, November 1892

Nietzsche, that strong enchanter ... Nietzsche completes
Blake and has the same roots. I have not read anything
with so much excitement since I got to love Morris's
stories which have the same curious astringent joy.

Letter to Lady Gregory, 1902

In [Ibsen's] *Rosmersholm* ... there is symbolism and a
stale odour of spilt poetry.

The Trembling of the Veil, 1922

[Oscar Wilde] was a parvenu, but a parvenu whose
whole bearing proved that if he did dedicate every story
in *A House of Pomegranates* to a lady of title, it was but to
show that he was Jack and the social ladder his
pantomime beanstalk.

Ib.

This is the first generation in which the spirit of
literature has been conquered by the spirit of the press,
of hurry, of immediate interests, and Bernard Shaw is
the Joseph whose prosperity has brought his brethren
into capivity.

Letter to Edmund Gosse, 1910

I agree about Shaw – he is haunted by the mystery he
flouts. He is an atheist who trembles in the haunted
corridor.

Letter to George Russell (AE), 1921

He loves all that has edge, all that is salt in the mouth, all
that is rough to the hand, all that heightens the emotions
by contest, all that strings into life the sense of tragedy
... I am certain that, in the long run, his grotesque plays
with their lyric beauty, their violent laughter, *The Playboy
of the Western World* most of all, will be loved for holding
so much of the mind of Ireland.

'J.M. Synge and the Ireland of his Time', 1910

And that enquiring man John Synge comes next,
That dying chose the living world for text
And never could have rested in the tomb
But that, long travelling, he had come
Towards nightfall upon certain set apart
In a most desolate stony place,
Towards nightfall upon a race
Passionate and simple like his heart.

'In Memory of Major Robert Gregory', 1918

[Synge] was the man that we needed, because he was
the only man I have ever known incapable of a political
thought or of a humanitarian purpose ... He was to do
for Ireland, though more by his influence on other
writers than by his direct influence, what Robert Burns
did for Scotland. 'The Irish Dramatic Movement', 1925

Synge's *Playboy* and O'Casey's *Plough and the Stars* were
attacked because ... they contain what a belief, tamed
down into a formula, shudders at, something wild and
ancient. 'The Irish Censorship', *Spectator*, 1928

I do not know whether Joyce's *Ulysses* is a great work of
literature. I have puzzled a great deal over that question
... All I will say is that it is the work of an heroic mind.

Senate Speech on Copyright Protection, 1927

The Irish literary revival

I feel more and more that we shall have a school of Irish
poetry – founded on Irish myth and history – a
neo-romantic movement.

Letter to Katharine Tynan, 1887

To the greater poets everything they see has its relation
to the national life, and through that to the universal and
divine life ... You can no more have the greater poetry
without a nation than religion without symbols. One can
only reach out to the universe with a gloved hand – that
glove is one's nation, the only thing one knows even a
little of.

'The Poet of Ballyshannon', *Providence Sunday Journal*, 1888

Much may depend in the future on Ireland now developing writers who know how to formulate in clear expressions the vague feelings now abroad – to formulate them for Ireland's, not for England's, use.

Letter to Katharine Tynan, 1889

Ireland is the true subject for the Irish.

'The Celt in London', *Boston Pilot*, 1889

There is no great nationality without literature, no great literature without nationality.   *Ib.*, 1890

Alone, perhaps, among the nations of Europe we are in our ballad or epic age ... Our poetry is still a poetry of the people in the main, for it still deals with the tales and thoughts of the people.

'Nationality and Literature: a lecture', 19 May 1893

The true ambition is to make criticism as international, and literature as National, as possible.

Letter to the Editor of *United Ireland*, 1894

We must be prepared to turn from a purely political nationalism with the land question as its lever, to a partly intellectual and historical nationalism like that of Norway, with the language question as its lever.

'Irish Language and Irish Literature', *The Leader*, 1900

I would ... speak to those who ... are convinced that art is tribeless, nationless, a blossom of No Man's Land. The Greeks looked within their borders ... I would have Ireland re-create the ancient arts, the arts as they were understood ... when they moved a whole people and not a few people who have grown up in a leisured class and made this understanding their business.

'Ireland and the Arts', 1901

The Gaelic movement is helping to preserve the national character of the people, and to prevent the country from becoming an imitation England. When an Irishman begins to resemble an Englishman, it is the very worst type that he resembles. It is not Shakespeare and Milton that have been superseding the Gaelic poets in Ireland, but the half-penny comics; in fact, Anglicisation has meant vulgarisation.

> 'The Gaelic Movement and the Parliamentary Party',
> *The Echo*, 1902

[W]hat is a National literature? ... It is the work of writers who are moulded by influences that are moulding their country, and who write out of so deep a life that they are accepted there in the end.

> 'First Principles', 1904

Have not all races had their first unity from a mythology that marries them to rock and hill?

> *The Trembling of the Veil*, 1922

Young Ireland had sought a nation unified by political doctrine alone, a subservient art and letters aiding and abetting ... All the past had been turned into melodrama with Ireland for blameless hero[...] and poet, novelist and historian had but one object, that we should hiss the villain, and only a minority doubted that the greater the talent the greater the hiss.   *Ib.*

The old literature of Ireland ... has been the chief illumination of my imagination all my life.

> Senate Speech on Irish Manuscripts, 1923

The modern literature of Ireland, and indeed all that stir of thought which prepared for the Anglo-Irish war, began when Parnell fell from power in 1891.

> 'The Irish Dramatic Movement', 1925

In Gaelic literature we have something that the English-speaking countries have never possessed – a great folk literature.

> 'The Child and the State: a lecture', 1925

You have disgraced yourselves again. Is this to be an ever-recurring celebration of the arrival of Irish genius? Synge first, and then O'Casey! The news of the happenings of the last few minutes will go from country to country. Dublin has once more rocked the cradle of genius. From such a scene in this theatre went forth the fame of Synge. Equally the fame of O'Casey is born here tonight. This is his apotheosis.

From the stage of the Abbey Theatre, during the first run of Sean O'Casey's *The Plough and the Stars*, 1927

Again and again I have defended plays or novels unlike anything I have myself attempted, or anything in the work of others that has given me great pleasure, because I have known that they were medicinal to a people struggling against second-hand thought and insincere emotion. 'The Great Blasket', *Spectator*, 1933

We will have no great popular literature until we get rid of the moral sycophants. Letter to Dorothy Wellesley, 1936

John Synge, I and Augusta Gregory thought
All that we did, all that we said or sang
Must come from contact with the soil, from that
Contact everything Antaeus-like grew strong.
We three in modern times alone had brought
Everything down to that sole test again,
Dream of the noble and the beggar-man.

'The Municipal Gallery Revisited', 1937

All that I have said and done,
Now that I am old and ill,
Turns into a question till
I lie awake night after night
And never get the answer right.
Did that play of mine send out
Certain men the English shot?
Did my words put too great strain
On that woman's reeling brain?
Could my spoken words have checked
That whereby a house lay wrecked?

'Man and the Echo', 1938

Irish poets, learn your trade,
Sing whatever is well made,
Scorn the sort now growing up
All out of shape from toe to top,
Their unremembering hearts and heads
Base-born products of base beds.
Sing the peasantry, and then
Hard-riding country gentlemen,
The holiness of monks, and after
Porter-drinkers' randy laughter;
Sing the lords and ladies gay
That were beaten into clay
Through seven heroic centuries;
Cast your mind on other days
That we in coming days may be
Still the Indomitable Irishry.

'Under Ben Bulben', 1938

The Theatre

I want to do a little play which can be acted and half
chanted and so help the return of bigger poetical plays
to the stage. This is really a magical revolution for the
magical word is the chanted word.

Letter to George Russell (AE), 1899

In London, where all the intellectual traditions gather to
die, men hate a play if they are told that it is literature,
for they will not endure a spiritual superiority; but in
Athens, where so many intellectual traditions were born,
Euripides once changed hostility to enthusiasm by
asking his playgoers whether it was his business to teach
them, or their business to teach him.

'The Theatre', February 1900

In Ireland, we had among our audience almost everybody who is making opinion in Ireland, who is a part of his time, and numbers went out of the playhouse thinking a little differently of that Ireland which their work is shaping: some went away angry, some delighted, but all had seen that upon the stage at which they could not look altogether unmoved.

Beltaine, April 1900

I would try and make a theatre where realism would be impossible. ... All the great poetic dramatists of the world wrote for a theatre that was half platform, half stage, and for actors that were, at least, as much orators as actors. *The United Irishman*, 1902

In Ireland, where the tide of life is rising, we turn ... to the imagination of the personality – to drama, gesture.

'First Principles', 1904

The quarrel of our Theatre today is the quarrel of the Theatre in many lands; for the old Puritanism, the old bourgeois dislike of power and reality have not changed, even when they are called by some Gaelic name. *The Arrow*, 1907

Tragedy is passion alone and, instead of character, it gets form from motives, the wandering of passion; while comedy is the clash of character. Eliminate character from comedy and you get farce. Farce is bound together by incident alone. (Eliminate passion from tragedy and you get melodrama.) 'Journal', January 1909

The Abbey Theatre will fail to do its full work because there is no accepted authority to explain why the more difficult pleasure is the nobler pleasure.

'Journal', March 1909

The new playwrights invent their subjects and dislike anything customary in the arrangement of the fable, but their expression is as common as the newspapers where they first learned to write.

'Journal', September 1909

My curse on plays
That have to be set up in fifty ways,
On the day's war with every knave and dolt,
Theatre business, management of men.
I swear before the dawn comes round again
I'll find the stable and pull out the bolt.
'The Fascination of What's Difficult', 1909-10

Once, when midnight smote the air,
Eunuchs ran through Hell and met
On every crowded street to stare
Upon great Juan riding by:
Even like these to rail and sweat
Staring upon his sinewy thigh.
'On those that hated *The Playboy of the Western World*, 1907', 1910

When we are high and airy hundreds say
That if we keep that flight they'll leave the place,
While those same hundreds mock another day
Because we have made our art of common things.
'At the Abbey Theatre (Imitated from Ronsard)', 1911

We have been the first to create a true 'People's Theatre',
and we have succeeded because it is not an exploitation
of local colour, [but] the making articulate of all the
dumb classes each with its own knowledge of the world,
its own dignity, but all objective with the objectivity of
the office and the workshop, of the newspaper and the
street, of mechanism and of politics.
'A People's Theatre: a letter to Lady Gregory',
The Irish Statesman, 1919

You and I and Synge, not understanding the clock, set
out to bring again the theatre of Shakespeare or rather
perhaps of Sophocles.
Ib.

I want to create for myself an unpopular theatre and an
audience like a secret society where admission is by
favour and never to many.
Ib.

We Cromwellian Directors laid down this principle
twenty-five years ago, and have not departed from it:
never accept or reject a play because of its opinions.

The Dublin Magazine, 1926

Dramatic action is a fire that must burn up everything
but itself ... Among the things that dramatic action must
burn up are the author's opinions; while he is writing he
has no business to know anything that is not a portion of
that action.

Letter to Sean O'Casey, 20 April 1928

Nothing was read in Ireland except newspapers,
prayer-books, popular novels; but if Ireland would not
read literature it might listen to it, for politics and the
Church had created listeners. I wanted a Theatre – I had
wanted it for years.

Dramatis Personae, 1935

I am a timid man except before a piece of paper or
rioters at the Abbey Theatre, and even there my courage
is limited to certain topics.

Introduction to *Essays and Introductions*, 1937

Players and painted stage took all my love,
And not those things that they were emblems of.

'The Circus Animals' Desertion', 1937-8

Ireland

I must learn to speak. A man must know how to speak
in Ireland just as a man in old times had to carry a
sword.

[*c*. 1888], 'Autobiography', *c*. 1916-17

All these good English Home Rule people, how they do patronise Ireland and the Irish. As if we were some new sort of deserving poor for whom bazaars and such like should be got up.

Letter to Ellen O'Leary, 1888

Cosmopolitanism is one of the worst [of Irish vices]. We are not content to dig our own potato patch in peace. We peer over the wall at our neighbour's instead of making our own garden green and beautiful. And yet it is a good garden and there have been great transactions within it.

'The Celt in London', *Boston Pilot*, 1890

In a battle, like Ireland's, which is one of poverty against wealth, one must prove one's sincerity by making oneself unpopular to wealth. One must accept the baptism of the gutter. Have not all teachers done the like?

Letter to Lady Gregory, 1900

I have always felt that my mission in Ireland is to serve taste rather than any definite propaganda.

Letter to Lady Gregory, 1901

In Ireland, where we have no mature intellectual tradition, and are in imperfect sympathy with the mature tradition of England, the only one we know anything of, we sometimes carry with us through our lives a defiant dogmatism like that of a clever schoolboy.

'John Eglinton', *The United Irishman*, 1901

Politics are, indeed, the forge in which nations are made, and the smith has been so long busy making Ireland according to His will that she may well have some important destiny.

'The Literary Movement in Ireland', 1901

It is a hard service they take that help me. Many that are red-cheeked now will be pale-cheeked; many that have been free to walk the hills and the bogs and the rushes will be sent to walk hard streets in far countries; many a good plan will be broken; many that have gathered money will not stay to spend it; many a child will be born and there will be no father at its christening to give it a name. They that have red cheeks will have pale cheeks for my sake, and for all that, they will think they are well paid.

> They shall be remembered for ever,
> They shall be alive for ever,
> They shall be speaking forever,
> The people shall hear them for ever.
>
> *Cathleen ni Houlihan*, 1902

When Spenser wrote of Ireland he wrote as an official, and out of the thoughts and emotions that had been organised by the State. He was the first of many Englishmen to see nothing but what he was desired to see.   'Edmund Spenser', October 1902

The root of it all is that the political class in Ireland ... have suffered through the cultivation of hatred as the one energy of their movement, a deprivation which is the intellectual equivalent to the removal of the genitals. Hence the shrillness of their voices. They contemplate all creative power as the eunuchs contemplate Don Juan as he passes through Hell on the white horse.

'Journal', March 1909

The soul of Ireland has become a vapour and her body a stone.   *Ib.*

In Ireland ... the cultivated remnant has no power on public opinion.   *Ib.*

There is a sinking away of national feeling which is very simple in its origin. You cannot keep the idea of a nation alive where there are no national institutions to reverence, no national success to admire, without a model of it in the mind of the people.   *Ib.*

The Irish people till they are better educated must
dream impermanent dreams, and if they do not find
them they will be ruined by the half-sirs with their
squalid hates and envies.

Ib.

The power of self-conquest, of elevation [in Ireland] has
been Protestant, and more or less a thing of class. All the
tragedians were Protestant – O'Connell was a comedian.
He had the gifts of the market place, of the clown at the
fair.

'Journal', April 1909

A zealous Irishman, especially if he lives out of Ireland,
spends his time in a never-ending argument about
Oliver Cromwell, the Danes, the penal laws, the
Rebellion of 1798, the famine, the Irish peasant, and ends
by substituting a traditional casuistry for a country.

'J.M. Synge and the Ireland of his Time', 1910

Go into Scotland again, or where you will, but begone
From this unlucky country that was made when the
    Devil spat.

The Green Helmet, 1910

Religious Ireland – and the pious Protestants of my
childhood were signal examples – thinks of divine
things as a round of duties separated from life and not
as an element that may be discovered in all circumstance
and emotion, while political Ireland sees the good
citizen but as a man who holds to certain opinions and
not as a man of good will.

Responsibilities, 1914

The Dublin tragedy has been a great sorrow and anxiety
… I am trying to write a poem on the men executed –
'terrible beauty has been born again' … I had no idea
that any public event could so deeply move me – and I
am very despondent about the future.

Letter to Lady Gregory, 11 May 1916

I have met them at the close of day
Coming with vivid faces
From counter or desk among grey
Eighteenth century houses.
I have passed with a nod of the head
Or polite meaningless words,
Or have lingered awhile and said
Polite meaningless words,
And thought before I had done
Of a mocking tale or a gibe
To please a companion
Around the fire at the club,
Being certain that they and I
But lived where motley is worn:
All changed, changed utterly:
A terrible beauty is born.

'Easter 1916', September 1916

Perhaps there is nothing so dangerous to a modern state,
when politics takes the place of theology, as a bunch of
martyrs. A bunch of martyrs (1916) were the bomb and
we are living in the explosion.

Letter to Olivia Shakespear, 9 October 1922

An infallible Church, with its mass in Latin and its
medieval philosophy, and our Protestant social
prejudice, have kept our ablest men from levelling
passions.   *The Trembling of the Veil*, 1922

We had fed the heart on fantasies,
The heart's grown brutal from the fare;
More substance in our enmities
Than in our love; O honey-bees,
Come build in the empty house of the stare.

'Meditations in Time of Civil War', 1923

If you show that this country, Southern Ireland, is going
to be governed by Catholic ideas and Catholic ideas
alone, you will never get the North. You will create an
impassable barrier between South and North ... You
will put a wedge into the midst of this nation.

Senate Speech on Divorce, 1925

Out of Ireland have we come.
Great hatred, little room,
Maimed us at the start.
I carry from my mother's womb
A fanatic heart.
                    'Remorse for Intemperate Speech', 1931

You must not believe what you read in the English
papers. They decide moral questions in the interests of
their parties and express their decisions with a
complacency that rouses other nations to fury. Here I
think we are genuinely troubled about right and wrong,
we don't decide easily. The hungry man is nearer to the
Saint than the full man.
                    Letter to Olivia Shakespear, 1933

It is amusing to live in a country where men will always
act. Where nobody is satisfied by thought.   *Ib.*

My father upon the Abbey stage, before him a raging
crowd:
'This land of saints,' and then as the applause died out,
'Of plaster saints'; his beautiful mischievous head
    thrown back.   'Beautiful Lofty Things', *c.* 1937

No people hate as we do in whom the past is always
alive ... I am joined to the 'Irishry' and expect a
counter-Renaissance.
                    'A General Introduction to My Work', 1937

I am no Nationalist, except in Ireland for passing reasons.
                                                        Ib.

When Pearse summoned Cuchulain to his side,
What stalked through the Post-Office? What intellect,
What calculation, number, measurement, replied?
We Irish, born into that ancient sect
But thrown upon this filthy modern tide
And by its formless spawning fury wrecked,
Climb to our proper dark, that we may trace
The lineaments of a plummet-measured face.
                    'The Statues', 1938

The Anglo-Irish

We against whom you have done this thing are no petty
people. We are one of the great stocks of Europe. We are
the people of Burke; we are the people of Grattan; we
are the people of Swift, the people of Emmet, the people
of Parnell. We have created the most of the modern
literature of this country. We have created the best of its
political intelligence.

Senate Speech on Divorce, 1925

They shall inherit my pride,
The pride of people that were
Bound neither to Cause nor to State,
Neither to slaves that were spat on,
Nor to the tyrants that spat,
The people of Burke and of Grattan
That gave, though free to refuse –
Pride like that of the morn,
When the headlong light is loose.

'The Tower', 1925

I declare this tower is my symbol; I declare
This winding, gyring, spiring treadmill of a stair is my
    ancestral stair;
That Goldsmith and the Dean, Berkeley and Burke have
    travelled there.   'Blood and the Moon', 1927

Intellectual Ireland was born when Berkeley wrote in
that famous notebook of his after an analysis of
contemporary mechanistic thought: 'We Irish do not
think so', or some such words.

'The Irish Censorship', *Spectator*, 1928

The other day I was asked why a certain man did not
live at Boar's Hill, the pleasant neighbourhood where so
many writers live, and replied, 'We Anglo-Irish hate to
surrender the solitude we have inherited', and then
began to wonder what I meant. I ran over the lives of my
friends, of Swift and Berkeley, and saw that all, as befits
scattered men in an ignorant country, were solitaries.

Preface to Oliver St John Gogarty's *Wild Apples*, 1930

I want Protestant Ireland to base some vital part of its
culture upon Burke, Swift and Berkeley.

Letter to Joseph Hone, 1930

Swift has sailed into his rest;
Savage indignation there
Cannot lacerate his breast.
Imitate him if you dare,
World-besotted traveller; he
Served human liberty.

'Swift's Epitaph', 1930

Whether they knew or not,
Goldsmith and Burke, Swift and the Bishop of Cloyne
All hated Whiggery; but what is Whiggery?
A levelling, rancorous, rational sort of mind
That looked out of the eye of a saint
Or out of drunkard's eye.

'The Seven Sages', 1931

From Jonathan Swift's dark grove he passed, and there
Plucked bitter wisdom that enriched his blood.

'Parnell's Funeral', 1933

Protestant Ireland had immense prestige ... [but] lacked
hereditary passion. Parnell, its last great figure, finding
that this lack had made the party of my father's old
friend Isaac Butt powerless, called in the peasants'
tenacity and violence.

Dramatis Personae, 1935

Old Man. Great people lived and died in this house;
    Magistrates, colonels, Members of Parliament,
    Captains and Governors, and long ago
    Men that fought at Aughrim and the Boyne.
    Some that had gone on Government work
    To London or to India came home to die,
    Or came from London every spring
    To look at the may-blossom in the park.
    They had loved the trees that he cut down
    To pay what he lost at cards
    Or spent on horses, drink and women;
    Had loved the house, had loved all
    The intricate passages of the house,
    But he killed the house; to kill a house
    Where great men grew up, married, died,
    I here declare a capital offence.

Purgatory, 1939

Religion & Mysticism

I was often devout, my eyes filling with tears at the
thought of God and of my own sins, but I hated church
... My father's unbelief had set me thinking about the
evidences of religion and I weighed the matter
perpetually with great anxiety, for I did not think that I
could live without religion.

Reveries over Childhood and Youth, 1914

One day some one spoke to me of the voice of the conscience, and as I brooded over the phrase I came to think that my soul, because I did not hear an articulate voice, was lost. I had some wretched days until being alone with one of my aunts I heard a whisper in my ear, 'What a tease you are!' At first I thought my aunt must have spoken, but when I found she had not, I concluded it was the voice of conscience and was happy again.

Ib.

Old Peasant. God forsakes us.
Cathleen. Old man, old man. He never closed a door
Unless one opened. I am desolate
Because of a strange thought that's in my heart;
But I have still my faith; therefore be silent;
For surely He does not forsake the world
But stands before it modelling in the clay
And moulding there His image. Age by age
The clay wars with his fingers and pleads hard
For its old, heavy, dull and shapeless ease;
But sometimes – though His hand is on it still –
It moves awry and demon hordes are born.

The Countess Cathleen, 1892

The Light of Lights
Looks always on the motive, not the deed,
The Shadow of Shadows on the deed alone.

Ib.

The Catholic religion likes to keep on good terms with its neighbours.

The Celtic Twilight, 1893

In Ireland this world and the world we go to after death are not far apart.

Ib.

It is not necessary to judge every one by the law, for we have also Christ's commandment of love.

The Tables of the Law, 1897

The only two powers that trouble the deeps are religion and love, the others make a little trouble upon the surface.

'A Symbolic Artist and the Coming of
Symbolic Art', *The Dome*, 1898

Without the arbitrary there cannot be religion.

'Journal', January 1909

We require a new statement of the moral doctrine, which shall be accepted by the average man, but which will at the same time be plainly beyond his power in practice. The Catholic Church created a system only possible for saints – hence its prolonged power.

Ib., March 1909

The education given by the Catholic schools seems to me to be in all matters of general culture a substituting of pedantry for taste.

Ib.

Now as at all times I can see in my mind's eye,
In their stiff, painted clothes, the pale unsatisfied ones …
            … hoping to find once more,
Being by Calvary's turbulence unsatisfied,
The uncontrollable mystery on the bestial floor.

'The Magi', 1913

We must not make a false faith by hiding from our thoughts the causes of doubt, for faith is the highest achievement of the human intellect, the only gift man can make to God, and therefore must be offered in sincerity.

Per Amica Silentia Lunae, 1917

Every child in growing from infancy to maturity should pass in imagination through the history of its own race and through something of the history of the world, and the most powerful part in that history is played by religion.

'The Child and the State: a lecture', 1925

In pity for man's darkening thought
He walked that room and issued thence
In Galilean turbulence;
The Babylonian starlight brought
A fabulous, formless darkness in;
Odour of blood when Christ was slain
Made all Platonic tolerance vain
And vain all Doric discipline.

The Resurrection, 1931

Irish Christianity is not gentle.

'The Mandukya Upanishad', 1935

My Christ, a legitimate deduction from the Creed of St
Patrick as I think, is that Unity of Being Dante compared
to a perfectly proportioned human body, Blake's
'Imagination', what the Upanishads have named 'Self'.

'A General Introduction to my Work', 1937

Come away, O human child!
To the waters and the wild
With a faery, hand in hand,
For the world's more full of weeping than you can
    understand.

'The Stolen Child', 1886

The mystical life is the very centre of all that I do and all
that I think and all that I write. It holds to my work the
same relation that the philosophy of Godwin held to the
work of Shelley and I have always considered myself a
voice of what I believe to be a greater renascence – the
revolt of the soul against the intellect – now beginning in
the world.

Letter to John O'Leary, 1892

Man ever journeys on with them
After the red-rose-bordered hem.
Ah, faeries, dancing under the moon,
A Druid land, a Druid tune!

'To Ireland in Coming Times', *c.* 1892

Come, faeries, take me out of this dull house!
Let me have all the freedom I have lost;
Work when I will and Idle when I will!
Faeries, come take me out of this dull world,
For I would ride with you upon the wind,
Run on the top of the dishevelled tide,
And dance upon the mountains like a flame.

The Land of Heart's Desire, 1894

Between my politics and my mysticism I shall hardly
have my head turned with popularity.

Letter to Lady Gregory, 1901

Am I a mystic? – no, I am a practical man. I have seen
the raising of Lazarus and the loaves and fishes and
have made the usual measurements, plummet line,
spirit level, and have taken the temperature by pure
mathematic.

Letter to Ethel Mannin, 1938

Realism & the Modern World

I hate journalists. There is nothing in them but tittering,
jeering emptiness. They have all made what Dante calls
the Great Refusal. That is, they have ceased to be
self-centred, have given up their individuality.

Letter to Katharine Tynan, 1888

Reason is the stopping of the pendulum, a kind of death.

'Journal', August 1910

Realism is created for the common people and was
always their peculiar delight, and it is the delight to-day
of all those whose minds, educated alone by
school-masters and newspapers, are without the
memory of beauty and emotional subtlety.

'Certain Noble Plays of Japan', 1916

'Though logic-choppers rule the town,
And every man and maid and boy
Has marked a distant object down,
An aimless joy is a pure joy,'
Or so did Tom O'Roughley say
That saw the surges running by,
'And wisdom is a butterfly
And not a gloomy bird of prey.'

'Tom O'Roughley', 1918

Locke sank into a swoon;
The Garden died;
God took the spinning-jenny
Out of his side.   'Fragments', 1931

I did not believe, nor do I now, that it is possible to
discover in the text-books of the schools, in the manuals
sold by religious booksellers, even in the subtle reverie
of saints, the most violent force in history.

Dramatis Personae, 1935

I go deeper than 'custom' for my convictions.
'A General Introduction to my Work', 1937

The realists turn our words into gravel, but the
musicians and the singers turn them into honey and oil
... You at any rate cannot sympathise with a horrible
generation that in childhood sucked Ibsen from Archer's
hygenic bottle.   *A Vision*, 1937

The woods of Arcady are dead,
And over is their antique joy;
Of old the world on dreaming fed;
Grey truth is now her painted toy.

'The Song of the Happy Shepherd' 1885

That leprosy of the modern – tepid emotions and many
aims. Many aims, when the greatest of the earth often
owned but two – fatherland and song.

'The Poetry of Sir Samuel Ferguson',
Dublin University Review, 1886

There are two boats going out to sea. In which shall we
sail? There is the little boat of science. Every century a
new little boat of science starts and is shipwrecked; and
yet again another puts forth, gaily laughing at its
predecessors. Then there is the great galleon of tradition,
and on it travel the great poets and dreamers of the past.
It was built long ago, nobody remembers when. From its
masthead flies the motto, *semper eadem*.

'Irish Wonders', *Providence Sunday Journal*, 1889

There's something every man has carried with him
And thought no more about than if it were
A mouthful of the wind; and now it's grown
A marketable thing! ...
'Go cry it all about the world', they said.
'Money for souls, good money for a soul.'

The Countess Cathleen, 1892

All life is revelation beginning in miracle and
enthusiasm, and dying out as it unfolds itself in what we
have mistaken for progress.

'The Theatre', February 1900

Our history speaks of opinions and discoveries, but in
ancient times ... history spoke of commandments and
revelations. They looked as carefully and as patiently
towards Sinai and its thunders as we look towards
parliaments and laboratories.   'Magic', 1901

The thoughts that we find for ourselves are timid and a
little secret, but those modern thoughts that we share
with large numbers are confident and very insolent. We
have little else to-day, and when we read our newspaper
and take up its cry, above all, its cry of hatred, we will
not think very carefully, because we hear the marching
feet.   'Edmund Spenser', October 1902

When there were no laws men warred on one another
and man to man, not with machines made in towns as
they do now, and they grew hard and strong in body.
They were altogether alive like Him that made them in
His image, like people in that unfallen country.

The Unicorn from the Stars, with Lady Gregory, 1908

The newspaper is the roar of the machine.

'Journal', January 1909

We, too, had good attendance once,
Hearers and hearteners of the work:
Aye, horsemen for companions,
Before the merchant and the clerk
Breathed on the world with timid breath.

'At Galway Races', 1908

What need you, being come to sense,
But fumble in the greasy till
And add the halfpence to the pence
And prayer to shivering prayer, until
You have dried the marrow from the bone?
For men were born to pray and save:
Romantic Ireland's dead and gone,
It's with O'Leary in the grave.

'September 1913'

Turning and turning in the widening gyre
The falcon cannot hear the falconer;
Things fall apart; the centre cannot hold;
Mere anarchy is loosed upon the world,
The blood dimmed tide is loosed, and everywhere
The ceremony of innocence is drowned;
The best lack all conviction, while the worst
Are full of passionate intensity.
Surely some revelation is at hand;
Surely the Second Coming is at hand ...
And what rough beast, its hour come round at last,
Slouches towards Bethlehem to be born?

'The Second Coming', 1919

Science has driven out the legends, stories, superstitions that protected the immature and the ignorant with symbol.

Introduction to *Fighting the Waves*, 1932

All's Whiggery now,
But we old men are massed against the world.

'The Seven Sages', 1931

When my generation denounced scientific humanitarian preoccupation, psychological curiosity, rhetoric, we had not found what ailed Victorian literature ... The mischief began at the end of the seventeenth century when man became passive before a mechanized nature.

Introduction to *The Oxford Book of Modern Verse*, 1936

After an age of necessity, truth, goodness, mechanism, science, democracy, abstraction, peace, comes an age of freedom, fiction, evil, kindred, art, aristocracy, particularity, war. Has our age burned to the socket?

'Stories of Michael Robartes and his Friends' in *A Vision*, 1937

When I stand upon O'Connell Bridge in the half-light and notice that discordant architecture, all those electric signs, where modern heterogeneity has taken physical form, a vague hatred comes up out of my own dark and I am certain that wherever in Europe there are minds strong enough to lead others the same vague hatred rises; in four or five or less generations this hatred will have issued in violence and imposed some kind of rule of kindred.

'A General Introduction to my Work', 1937

Old Man. I have been asked to produce a play called *The Death of Cuchulain*. It is the last of a series of plays which has for theme his life and death. I have been selected because I am out of fashion and out of date like the antiquated romantic stuff the thing is made of ... I am sure that as I am producing a play for people I like, it is not probable, in this vile age, that they will be more in number than those who listened to the first performance of Milton's *Comus* ... If there are more than a hundred I won't be able to escape people who are educating themselves out of the Book Societies and the like, sciolists all, pickpockets and opinionated bitches.

The Death of Cuchulain, 1939

Politics & War

Out of the ideas and emotions of the average man you can make no better thing than good rhetoric.

'Young Ireland', *The Bookman*, January 1897

Yours is patriotism of the fine sort – patriotism that lays burdens upon a man, and not the patriotism that takes burdens off. The British press just now, as I think, only understands the other sort, the sort that makes a man say 'I need not trouble to get wisdom, for I am English and my vices have made me great'.

Letter to Henry Newbolt, 1902

I fear the representatives of the collective opinion.

'Journal', December 1908, *Memoirs*

Too long a sacrifice
Can make a stone of the heart.

'Easter 1916', September 1916

I think we should put aside once and for all, all
diplomacy in dealing with the people of the country. We
have been diplomatised for a generation. Let us stop it.
Senate Speech on the Election of a Chairman, 1922

This Country will not always be an uncomfortable place
for a country gentleman to live in, and it is most
important that we should keep in this country a certain
leisured class ... On this matter I am a crusted Tory. I am
of the opinion of the ancient Jewish book which says
'there is no wisdom without leisure'.
Senate Speech on Damage to Property, 1923

I do not think that there is any statesman in Europe who
would not have gladly accepted the immorality of the
renaissance if he could be assured of his country
possessing the genius of the renaissance. Genius has its
virtue, and it is only a small blot on the escutcheon if it is
sexually irregular.   Senate Speech on Divorce, 1925

Every political party had the same desire to substitute
for life, which never does the same thing twice, a bundle
of reliable principles and assertions.
'The Irish Dramatic Movement', 1925

I think we should not lose sight of the simple fact that it
is more desirable and more important to have able men
in this House than to get representative men into this
House.
Senate Speech on Senate Membership, 1928

Do not be elected to the Senate of your country. I think
myself, after six years, well out of that of mine. Neither
you nor I, nor any other of our excitable profession, can
match those old lawyers, old bankers, old business men,
who, because all habit and memory, have begun to
govern the world.   'To Ezra Pound', 1928

History is very simple – the rule of the many, then the
rule of the few, day and night, night and day for ever,
while in small disturbed nations day and night race.
Letter to Olivia Shakespear, 1933

What if the Church and the State
Are the mob that howls at the door!
Wine shall run thick to the end,
Bread taste sour.   'Church and State', 1934

Fascist, nationalist, clerical, anti-clerical, are all
responsible according to the number of their victims. I
have not been silent; I have used the only vehicle I
possess – verse.
                    Letter to Ethel Mannin, 1936

I have a horror of modern politics – I see nothing but the
manipulation of popular enthusiasm by false news.
                    Letter to Ethel Mannin, 1937

What discords will drive Europe to that artificial unity –
only dry or drying sticks can be tied into a bundle –
which is the decadence of every civilisation?
                    A Vision, 1937

Hurrah for revolution and more cannon-shot!
A beggar upon horseback lashes a beggar on foot.
Hurrah for revolution and cannon come again!
The beggars have changed places, but the lash goes on.
                    'The Great Day', 1937

A statesman is an easy man,
He tells his lies by rote;
A journalist makes up his lies
And takes you by the throat;
So stay at home and drink your beer
And let the neighbours vote,
          Said the man in the golden breastplate
          Under the old stone cross.
                    'The Old Stone Cross', 1937

How can I, that girl standing there,
My attention fix
On Roman or on Russian
Or on Spanish politics?
Yet here's a travelled man that knows
What he talks about,
And there's a politician
That has read and thought,
And maybe what they say is true
Of war and wars alarms,
But O that I were young again
And held her in my arms.

'Politics', 1938

I know that I shall meet my fate
Somewhere among the the clouds above;
Those that I fight I do not hate,
Those that I guard I do not love;
My country is Kiltartan Cross,
My countrymen Kiltartan's poor,
No likely end could bring them loss
Or leave them happier than before.
Nor law, nor duty bade me fight,
Nor public men, nor cheering crowds,
A lonely impulse of delight
Drove to this tumult in the clouds;
I balanced all, brought all to mind,
The years to come seemed waste of breath,
A waste of breath the years behind
In balance with this life, this death.

'An Irish Airman Foresees his Death', 1918

An affable Irregular,
A heavily-built Falstaffian man,
Comes cracking jokes of civil war
As though to die by gunshot were
The finest play under the sun.

The Road at My Door, 'Meditations in Time of Civil War', 1923

'Love war because of its horror, that belief may be changed, civilisation renewed. We desire belief and lack it. Belief comes from shock and is not desired. When a kindred discovers through apparition and horror that the perfect cannot perish nor even the imperfect long be interrupted, who can withstand that kindred? Belief is renewed continually in the ordeal of death.'

'Stories of Michael Robartes and his Friends', *A Vision*, 1937

Epigraph

Under bare Ben Bulben's head
In Drumcliff churchyard Yeats is laid.
An ancestor was rector there
Long years ago, a church stands near,
By the road an ancient cross.
No marble, no conventional phrase;
On limestone quarried near the spot
By his command these words are cut:
      Cast a cold eye
      On life, on death
      Horseman pass by!

'Under Ben Bulben', 4 September 1938